1960s Racing Car

D0183344

Viking Longship

American Train

Spy Plane

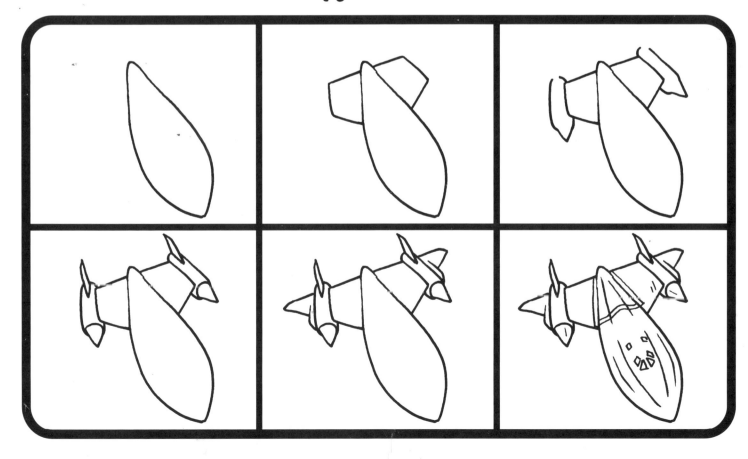

Formula 1 Racing car

Road Roller

Cruise Ship

Chopper Bike

747 Jumbo Jet

Custom Car

Mini

Digger

Lifeboat

Helicopter

Ski-Doo

Moon Buggy

Crane

TGV Train

combine Harvester

Racing Motorbike

Police car

Wright Brothers' Flyer

Mini Digger

Jet Ski

Space Shuttle

Chinese Junk Ship

Land Rover

Bullet Train

Motocross Bike

Traction Engine

Stealth fighter

The first car

Dumper

Cadillac

Motorised Rickshaw

Hydro-foil

Snow Plough Engine

Spitfire

Bubble car

cement Truck

Microlight

Paddle Steamer

17th Century Ship

Monster Truck

Dumper Truck

Scooter

Le Mans Racing car

Skip Truck

Hovercraft

The Mallard Train

Roller

Fishing Boat

Pick-up Truck

Lorry

Speed Boat

1901 oldsmobile

Sea Plane

London Bus

Tractor

Snow cat

Fire Engine

Stock car

Thrust II

Tug Boat

The Rocket

Citroen 2CV

Quad Bike

London Taxi

Coach

Submersible

1920s Motorbike

Concept Electric Car

Bulldozer

4x4 off-Road Vehicle

Rolls Royce

Light Aircraft

Dragster

Wild West Train

Model T ford

Dune Buggy

Gossamer Albatross

Fork Lift Truck

concorde

Stretch Limo

Yacht

Jeep

Submarine

Bi-Plane

Monorail Train

cable car

Sunray

Airship

VW Beetle

Transit Van

Hang-glider

funicular

Rocket

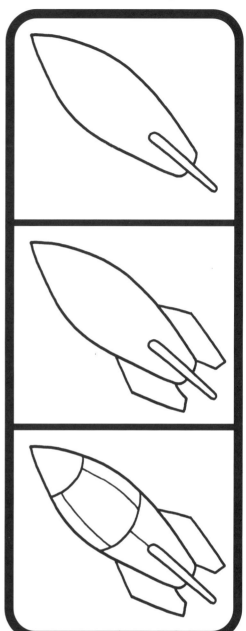

Lindbergh's 'Spirit of St Louis'

Glider

Tram

Bell X-1 Rocket